MACMILLAN READERS

ELEMENTARY LEVEL

The Beginning of Everything Else

Novelization by Jennifer Baker

Based on the television series "Dawson's Creek™"
created by and episodes
"Dawson's Creek™" and "Dance"
written by Kevin Williamson

This specially retold version by F. H. Cornish

GW00702893

MACMILLAN

Founding Editor: John Milne

The Macmillan Readers provide a choice of enjoyable reading materials for learners of English. The series is published at six levels – Starter, Beginner, Elementary, Pre-intermediate, Intermediate and Upper.

Level control
Information, structure and vocabulary are controlled to suit the students' ability at each level.

The number of words at each level:

Starter	about 300 basic words
Beginner	about 600 basic words
Elementary	about 1100 basic words
Pre-intermediate	about 1400 basic words
Intermediate	about 1600 basic words
Upper	about 2200 basic words

Vocabulary
Some difficult words and phrases in this book are important for understanding the story. Some of these words are explained in the story and some are shown in the pictures. From Pre-intermediate level upwards, words are marked with a number like this: ...^{3}. These words are explained in the Glossary at the end of the book.

Contents

	A Note About This Story	4
	The People in This Story	6
	A Picture Dictionary	8
1	Everything Changes	10
2	A New Girl in Town	18
3	Capeside High	22
4	At the Movie Theater	29
5	Almost a Kiss	33
6	The Kissing Lesson	38
7	A Change of Plan	41
8	At The Dance	46
9	The Beginning of Everything Else	52
	Points for Understanding	57

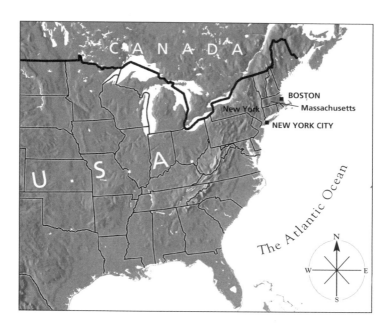

A Note About This Story

Kevin Williamson is a screenplay writer and a producer and director of movies. He was born on March 14th, 1965 and grew up in New Bern, a small town in the state of North Carolina, in the east of the U.S.A.

Kevin loved movies and his favorite director was Steven Speilberg. Kevin studied theater and film at East Carolina University. In 1987, he left New Bern and went to New York. He wanted to become an actor. When he went to Los Angeles a few years later, he worked as an assistant to a director of music videos. Kevin studied script writing and wrote screenplays for movies. The first successful movie that he wrote was *Scream* (1996). Paul Stupin worked for Columbia TriStar Television. He read the screenplay for *Scream* and he liked it. He asked Kevin to write a TV show. Kevin thought about his life in his small home town and he wrote the story for "Dawson's Creek™". The first episode of the show was made in 1997. Paul Stupin was the Executive Producer of "Dawson's Creek™".

Kevin wrote the screenplays for the movies *Scream 2* (1997), *I Know What You Did Last Summer* (1997) and *The Faculty* (1998). He wrote and directed the movie, *Teaching Mrs Tingle* (1999) and he produced the movie *Scream 3* in 2000.

The story of "**Dawson's Creek™**" takes place in a small town in the state of Massachusetts, in the northeast of the United States. The small towns and villages on the east coast have many visitors during the summer months. The tourists go fishing and they visit the restaurants. They play water sports on the sea and on the small rivers—the creeks—in the area. "Dawson's Creek™" is based on Kevin Williamson's own life when he was a teenager. He called the town in his story Capeside. The characters of Dawson and Joey are based on Kevin himself and his best friend, Fanny Norwood.

Jennifer Baker lives in New York City with her husband and her son. She has written more than thirty novels for young readers. She has also written scripts and material for websites.

———

script the words of a movie that actors have to speak.
screenplay the script of a movie that includes all the important information for everyone who is making the movie. For example, there are instructions for the actors, cameramen and film technicians. There are descriptions of where the scenes take place.
director the person who gives instructions to everyone as a scene is filmed. The director also decides how the movie is edited before it is shown to audiences.
producer the person who is responsible for getting the money to make a movie.

The People in This Story

Dawson Leery
Age: 15
Hair: blond
Eyes: light brown
A student at Capeside High School

Family
Father: Mr Mitch (Mitchell) Leery—an architect
Mother: Mrs Gale Leery—a news presenter at a TV station

Joey (Josephine) Potter
Age: 15
Hair: long, dark brown
Eyes: brown
A student at Capeside High School

Family
Father: Mr Mike Potter—in jail
Mother: Mrs Lily Potter—dead
Sister: Bessie. Bessie and her boyfriend, Bodie, work in "The Ice House" café.
Nephew: Alexander—Bessie and Bodie's son

Pacey Witter
Age: 15
Hair: dark brown
Eyes: brown
A student at Capeside High School

Family
Father: Mr John Witter—Capeside's Chief Police Officer
Mother: Mrs Mary Witter

Brother: Doug Witter—Capeside's Deputy Police Officer
Sisters: 3

Jen (Jennifer) Lindley
Age: 15
Hair: blond
Eyes: blue
A student at Capeside High School

Family
Father: Mr Theodore Lindley—lives in New York
Mother: Mrs Helen Lindley—lives in New York
Grandmother: "Grams" (Mrs Evelyn Ryan)
Grandfather: "Gramps" (Mr Joseph Ryan)

Tamara Jacobs
Age: late 30s
Hair: long, blond
Eyes: light brown with long, dark eyelashes
She is the English teacher at Capeside High School.

Cliff Elliott
Age: 17
Hair: brown
Eyes: gray
A student at Capeside High School. He is the best player on the football team.

Ben Gold
He is the teacher of the film class at Capeside High School.

A Picture Dictionary

view-finder

video camera

case

video tape

box of popcorn

movie theater

creek

dock

oars

rowboat

harbor

fishing boats

pleasure boats

boardwalk

dining hall

loudspeaker

students' lockers

classroom

gymnasium

1

Everything Changes

"Dawson, I will *not* kiss Pacey Witter!" Joey Potter said angrily.

The girl who spoke was tall and pretty and she had long brown hair. The boy who she was speaking to was blond and handsome. He had light brown eyes and a fine mouth. Joey Potter and Dawson Leery had been friends all their lives. Each was the other's best friend. But they were both fifteen years old. And life gets difficult for girls and boys at that age.

The person who Joey didn't want to kiss wasn't looking at the other two. He was looking out over the water of the little creek. Pacey Witter was fifteen too. He had short brown hair and long arms and legs. Pacey wasn't ugly—he was quite good-looking. But he didn't look like Dawson.

Pacey was a nice person. He was funny. People laughed at his jokes. But he tried to make everyone like him, and he tried too hard. He was trying too hard to grow up. Pacey had friends, but most of the time, he felt lonely. He felt ugly and lonely and stupid. He didn't want to be fifteen.

Pacey was often nervous with girls. When he was with girls, he always did the wrong thing. And when he spoke to them, he always said the wrong thing. Fifteen is a difficult age for everyone, but Pacey had more problems than most fifteen-year-olds.

Pacey's family didn't understand him. Pacey's father was the Chief of Police in Capeside. Pacey's brother was a police officer too. They were tough men. They didn't understand Pacey and they didn't like him.

Why did Dawson want Joey to kiss Pacey? Because Dawson was making a horror movie. Dawson had written the screenplay for the movie. And he was the cameraman and the director too. He operated the video camera. He told the actors what to do. And his friends Joey and Pacey were the actors in his movie. In the movie, Pacey was an evil teenage killer. Joey was a teenage girl who falls in love with the killer.

It was now Saturday morning, and Dawson was trying to shoot some important scenes for his film. It was the last weekend of a school vacation. Dawson wanted to finish the film soon. Everything had been OK until today. But in the scene which they were shooting now, Pacey had to kiss Joey.

"Dawson, you *have* to change this scene!" Joey said.

"I *can't* change this scene, Joey," Dawson said. "You *have* to kiss him. That's in the story. And the people who see the film have to believe in this kiss. It has to look like a *real* kiss. You don't have to touch Pacey's lips with your lips—you don't have to do it for real. But you need to bring your lips very close to his. Then the scene will look good in the movie. People will think, 'She kissed him.' That's all that I want."

Joey pointed her hand at Pacey.

"This—this *person* won't do it that way," she said angrily. "He always tries to kiss me for real. He always tries to put his lips on mine. And I *hate* it!"

Joey and Pacey were friends. She had known him for many years. But she didn't like being close to him. When he tried to kiss her, her body felt cold and then hot. She felt ill. She was *not* going to kiss Pacey. Dawson was Joey's best friend. But she wasn't going to do *this* for him!

"OK," said Dawson. "We won't shoot any more scenes today."

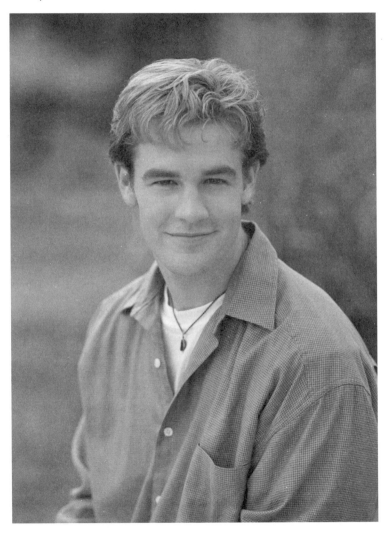

"I have to work on your head this afternoon, Joey," Dawson said.

In the last scene of Dawson's horror film, Pacey, "The Evil Teenager," was going to cut off Joey's head. Dawson wanted the scene to look real. So he was making a model of Joey's head. Pacey was going to hold up the model head in the last shot of the movie. Dawson was making the model head from rubber. He had taken lots of photos of Joey. Photos of her face, photos of the back of her head, and photos of the sides of her face. This afternoon, he was going to make the rubber head look more like the photos.

Dawson put his video camera in its case.

"I'll see you this evening, Joey," he said. "I've borrowed videos of some great movies."

———

The three friends had lived in the little Massachusetts town of Capeside all their lives. Pacey lived by the sea, in the largest part of the quiet town. His home was near the harbor. Dawson lived near the creek. Joey lived in a small wooden house on the other side of the creek. The creek flowed through the town and out into the sea.

Dawson's family was rich. They lived in a beautiful house. Dawson's father was an architect—he designed buildings. Most of the buildings that Mitchell Leery designed were hotels and expensive restaurants. Dawson's mother, Gale, worked at the Capeside television station. She worked on the TV news programs. Every evening, Dawson could see his mother on TV. Every evening, Mrs Leery read the news and talked to other news reporters about the day's stories.

Dawson had always learned about life from TV. Maybe that's why he loved movies.

Dawson had always loved watching movies. After school, and on weekends, he worked in a video rental store in Capeside. The store was named Screenplay Video. Pacey worked there too. But Pacey worked there because he wanted to earn money. Dawson worked at the store because the owner let him borrow videos. Almost every evening, Dawson watched videos of great movies from the past. He learned so much from them. His favorite film director was Steven Spielberg. He had watched Spielberg's films hundreds of times.

Dawson wanted to make his own movies. His parents helped him. They gave him a video camera. He spent a lot of time writing scripts. The short movie that he was making now was very important to him. Every year there was a film festival in Boston—the largest city in the state of Massachusetts. And every year at the festival, there was a competition for young film directors. Young people, who were students at schools in the state, sent their short movies to the festival. A famous film director chose the best movie. There was a prize for the best film. Dawson wanted to win the prize this year.

Dawson had a good life. His parents loved him very much, and he loved them. He was their only child. Dawson had no brothers or sisters.

Joey Potter's life wasn't as good as Dawson's life. Joey lived with her older sister, Bessie. Their house wasn't beautiful. The paint on the house was old and the colors were no longer bright. The Potters couldn't do anything about this. They didn't have much money. Joey and Bessie's mother was dead. Their father had left their home when the children were very young. And now he was in jail.

The Potters owned a café in the town. It was named

The Ice House. Bessie worked at the café and her boyfriend worked there too. Joey worked at The Ice House on the weekends and she worked there in the evenings, after school.

Joey loved her sister, but they weren't always happy when they were together. Soon, Bessie was going to have a baby. Bessie was tired most of the time. She often felt ill. And when she felt ill she became angry with Joey. Lots of things in Joey's life were not good. The best thing in her life was her friendship with Dawson Leery.

―――――

It was now Saturday evening. Dawson and Joey were watching videos in Dawson's room. They always did this on Saturday evenings. Joey didn't work at the café on Saturday evenings. When the weather was good, she crossed the creek to Dawson's house in her little rowboat. That was quicker than using the road. For many years, the evenings had always ended the same way. Joey didn't go back to her own house. She stayed with Dawson. The two of them slept in Dawson's big bed. This had never been a problem for them. But tonight, Joey was worried.

The last video finished.

"I must go home now," Joey said. "I'm tired. We have to shoot more scenes for the movie tomorrow morning. I have to work in the afternoon, and school starts again on Monday."

"Stay here tonight," Dawson said. "You always stay here on Saturday nights."

Joey looked at her friend sadly. "Dawson, we're growing up," she said. "Our bodies are changing. Our feelings are changing—well, my feelings are changing. We can't sleep in the same bed any more."

"We slept in the same bed last week," Dawson replied. "Why is this week different?"

"Everything changes, Dawson," Joey said. It was so difficult to tell him about her feelings.

"Nothing *has* to change," Dawson said. Now he was sad too. "I want everything to be the same as it has always been."

"Dawson," Joey said quietly. "I've known you since we were little children. I've always loved you as a friend. But now, our relationship has to change. I'm beginning to love you in a different way. I'm nearly a woman now. You're nearly a man. We're growing up fast. I'm starting to love you differently. I'm starting to love you in a grown-up way. Do you understand? Do you love me in that way too? Dawson, do you want me to be your girlfriend?"

"No, Joey," Dawson said. "I don't want you to be my girlfriend. I want you to be my *special* friend—my best friend. I want to talk to you about everything in my life. I want to talk about my hopes, fears and troubles. I don't want to grow up if I lose you as my special friend."

"Oh, Dawson," Joey said. "Your life is a movie. That's what you think. You always want a happy ending. But you can't write the script for other people's lives. You can't make everything simple and happy. Life is difficult."

"So, is this the end of our friendship, Joey?" Dawson asked unhappily. "Is this the end of everything?"

"No, Dawson, this is only the end of one thing," Joey replied. "It's the end of something that was simple. It's the end of our lives as children. It's the beginning of everything else. Life *doesn't* end like a movie, my friend! Life goes on, day after day."

2

A New Girl in Town

The next morning, Dawson, Joey and Pacey were shooting some more scenes for Dawson's movie. They were filming at the edge of the creek, near Dawson's house.

Dawson didn't ask Joey to kiss Pacey again.

"We'll shoot that scene next week," he told them. "In the next scene—" He stopped talking.

A taxi had stopped outside the house that was next to Dawson's house. A very beautiful girl got out of the taxi. She had blond hair and she was wearing lovely, expensive clothes. She was about the same age as the three friends.

"What a wonderful girl!" Pacey said.

Dawson didn't reply. There was nothing to say. Suddenly, Dawson was in love. He'd seen the girl before—he was sure of that. Who was she? Then he remembered who she was. An old couple—Mr and Mrs Ryan—lived in the house next to Dawson's house. And this girl was their granddaughter, Jennifer Lindley. She didn't live in Capeside. She lived in New York City with her parents. Sometimes she visited her grandparents. But she hadn't looked like this when she had last visited. She was growing up fast!

The driver of the taxi took lots of bags and cases out of the car. He put them on the ground. Then he got back into the taxi and drove away. The beautiful blond girl walked over to the edge of the creek.

"Hi," she said. "I'm Jen Lindley. I've come to stay with my grandparents."

Dawson, Pacey, and Joey told the girl their names.

"Hi," she said. "I'm Jen Lindley."

"Will this be a long visit?" Dawson asked. "You have a lot of bags and cases."

"Yes," Jen replied. "I don't know when I'll go back to New York. Gramps—my grandfather—is very ill. I'm going to help my grandmother. We'll take care of him together. Maybe it will be a *very* long visit. I'm going to start school here tomorrow—at Capeside High."

Dawson and Pacey smiled at each other. Capeside High was their school. Joey was a student there too.

Dawson and Pacey smiled. But Joey didn't smile. She was looking at Dawson. And Dawson was looking into the beautiful eyes of this new girl from New York. Joey understood what was happening. She was losing Dawson's friendship and she was very sad.

———

That afternoon, Dawson and Pacey were working at Screenplay Video. The store wasn't very busy. Dawson was putting videos on shelves. Pacey was standing behind the customer desk. He was waiting for someone to rent a video. But maybe nobody wanted a movie on this Sunday afternoon.

Suddenly the door opened and a woman walked into the store. Her blond hair was very long and her black dress was very short. She was the most beautiful woman that Pacey had ever seen. She was much older than him but she was gorgeous.

"Hello," Pacey said quickly. "Can I help you? My name is Pacey."

"Hi, Pacey," the woman said in a soft voice. "I'm Tamara. I've only been in this town a few days. I have a new job here. I start work tomorrow. I want to rent a video for the evening."

Pacey gave the woman a piece of paper.

"Please write your name and address on this form, then you can rent a video," he told her.

The woman filled in the form.

"You can look at the videos on the shelves," Pacey said. "But maybe you know which video you want. If you do, tell me the title. I'll find it for you."

"I want to rent *The Graduate*, if you have it," the woman said. And she gave Pacey a lovely smile. "Have you seen that movie?" the woman went on. "It's about a young man who falls in love with an older woman."

Pacey couldn't speak for a moment. His face became red. Was this woman telling him something? Was she flirting with him?

"Y–yes, that's a great film," Pacey said, when he could speak. "We have that. But have you seen the movie *Summer of '42?*"

"What's the movie about?" The woman asked. She had light brown eyes and long dark eyelashes.

"It's about an older woman who falls in love with a teenage boy—a boy who is becoming a man," Pacey replied. "It's a great movie!"

"Yes, I remember it now. *Summer of '42* was a great movie," Tamara said. "It was once my favorite film." She laughed. "I'll rent that movie another day. I like those kinds of movies. But I'll take *The Graduate* for this evening."

Pacey walked over to one of the tall shelves and took down a video. He gave it to Tamara.

"How much is the rental cost?" she asked.

"You can pay when you return the video," Pacey said. "Please come back soon."

"Yes, I'll come back soon," the woman said. "Thanks for all your help." And she smiled at him again. "Goodbye, Pacey."

"Did you hear that?" Pacey asked Dawson when the woman had left the store. "Tamara wants me! She was flirting with me."

"You're wrong Pacey. You're dreaming," Dawson replied, smiling. "She was laughing at you, Pacey. Tamara will *not* be interested in a high school student."

3

Capeside High

On Monday morning, Jen Lindley walked to school with Dawson. It was her first day at Capeside High. She was friendly and she was intelligent. After half an hour, Dawson thought, "I've known her all my life. I've been waiting for her all my life. She's wonderful." When classes began, Dawson had to go to a different classroom. He was sad to leave her.

During the morning, Dawson attended a film class. The teacher was Mr Gold. He was a pleasant, middle-aged man. His glasses hung from a chain around his neck.

The class was about the history of movies. But each year, the school also helped one student who wanted to make a movie. The school sponsored the film—it paid the cost of making it. And the school sent the movie to Boston, for the competition for young directors. Mr Gold always helped the student who was making the film.

Dawson wanted Capeside High to sponsor his film, but

that wasn't going to happen. Most of the students who attended the film class were older than Dawson. It was always one of the older students whose film was sponsored.

"You must wait until you're older," Mr Gold told Dawson. "Maybe we'll sponsor a movie for you another year."

But when Dawson heard about the film that the school *was* going to sponsor, he was angry. The student who was making it was named Cliff Elliot. He was a tall, handsome seventeen-year-old boy. Cliff had brown hair, gray eyes and a big, muscular body. He was the best player on the school football team. All the girls liked him. And his movie was going to be about football. It was going to be about a tall handsome boy who was a member of a school football team!

"This movie will be so boring," Dawson thought. "Why is the school going to spend money on something stupid? Why isn't it helping a great new director at the beginning of his life in movies? Why isn't it helping *me*?"

————

Pacey walked into the room where his English class was going to take place. And he had a surprise. A beautiful blond woman was standing behind the teacher's desk. It was Tamara—the gorgeous woman who had rented *The Graduate* at Screenplay Video!

Pacey walked over to her and smiled.

"Hi, Tamara," he said. "It's good to see you. What are *you* doing here?"

"Hello, Pacey," the woman replied. "I work here. If you're a member of this class, I'm your new English teacher. It's good to see you too, but you must call me Miss Jacobs when we're in school."

"Oh, maybe I'll see you—"

Miss Jacobs held up her hand.

"Please sit down now, Pacey," she said. "I want to start the class."

———

During the English class, Pacey was thinking. But he wasn't thinking about English poetry. He was thinking about the teacher.

"She likes me," he told himself. "She really likes me. Dawson was wrong. She *was* flirting with me yesterday. She doesn't think, 'He's a stupid, ugly kid.' She really wants to know me. OK, she's my teacher. Is that my fault? Is that *her* fault? No! She wants me and I'm going to talk to her again."

At the end of the class, he walked over to the teacher's desk. "Hi, Tamara—Miss Jacobs," he said. "Did you enjoy *The Graduate?*"

"Yes, it was great," she replied.

"Do you want to rent *Summer of '42* tonight?" he asked. "That's the kind of movie that you like. And the store is open until eight thirty."

"No, I don't want to rent a video tonight," Miss Jacobs replied. "There's a new movie at the theater here in town. I'm going to see that tonight. It starts at nine o'clock."

At lunchtime, Jen looked for Joey in the dining hall. She found her quickly and sat down at her table.

"Joey, I want to ask you something. It's something important," Jen said. "It's about Dawson. Is he your boyfriend?"

"No," Joey replied. "He isn't my boyfriend. He's someone who I've known all my life. But he isn't my boyfriend."

She stopped speaking for a moment.

"Jen, Dawson is a good person," Joey went on. "He hasn't been in love before. Be careful with him. Please don't hurt him."

"I won't hurt him, Joey," Jen said. "I want to be his friend. And I want to be your friend too."

Now Jen stopped for a moment.

"Joey," she went on. "My grandmother said some strange things about you—about you and your family."

"Oh, lots of people in this town say strange things about us," Joey replied. Her voice was cold and hard. "What *did* she say?"

"Grams said, 'Don't talk to Joey Potter. Stay away from her and her sister.' Why doesn't my grandmother like you?" Jen asked.

"Well, my father is in jail," Joey said. "He steals things. And my sister is going to have a baby and she isn't married. And her boyfriend, Bodie, is black. There aren't many African-American people in Capeside."

"What happened to your mother?" Jen asked.

"She died," Joey said. "Well, people say strange things about the Potter family. Maybe you can understand why now. Does it worry you?"

Jen laughed.

"No," she replied. "People said strange things about me when I lived in New York. Your family sounds great!"

Jen got up and left the table.

"She's trying to be nice to me," Joey thought. "But I don't want anyone else to love Dawson."

———

At another table, Pacey was talking to Dawson.

"You *have* to come with me, Dawson," he said. "You have to come to the movie theater tonight. We can go after the video store closes. Tamara asked me to meet her at the theater. But I need a friend there too. It's going to be the best evening of my life."

"Pacey, you've made a mistake," Dawson said. "Teachers don't go to movies with students."

"You don't understand. She wants me—I know that!" Pacey told him.

Before the afternoon classes started, Dawson found Jen. She was taking some school books from her locker.

"Jen, Pacey wants to go to a movie tonight," Dawson said. "He wants me to go with him. Will you come too? It will be fun."

"Yes, OK, that will be great," Jen replied. Then she closed the metal door and locked it.

"I'll meet you at eight forty," Dawson said.

———

After school finished for the day, Dawson met Joey. They walked together down to the creek and sat down near the water.

"Joey, will you come to a movie tonight?" Dawson asked. "I've made a date with Jen. I've asked Jen to go to a movie with me. But Pacey will be at the movie theater too. Two boys and one girl—that will be difficult. It will be much better if you come. You can talk to Pacey."

Joey turned and looked at Dawson.

"You want me to come to a movie and talk to Pacey," she said slowly. "You want *me* to make a date with *Pacey Witter* this evening? You want me to do that while you flirt with Jen. Is that right, Dawson?"

Dawson looked unhappy.

"Well, yes," he said.

"I have a choice," Joey said. "I can go to the movie with you and Jen and Pacey. Or I can jump into the creek and kill myself. OK, I'll jump into the creek! It will be much more fun. You're crazy, Dawson!"

"Joey, please do this for me," Dawson said. "You're my best friend. Don't you want to help me?"

"No," Joey replied and she turned her face away.

"Oh, *please*, Joey. Please, please, please, *please*!"

Joey looked at her friend again.

"Dawson, I wouldn't do this for anyone else in the world," she said. "OK, I'll see you tonight."

Dawson walked towards his house and Joey got into her rowboat.

As she rowed across the creek, Joey thought about Jen Lindley.

"I hate her," she told herself. "I hate her smile. I hate her blond hair. I hate her expensive clothes. I hate her!"

"Joey, please do this for me," Dawson said.
"You're my best friend. Don't you want to help me?"

4

At the Movie Theater

At eight thirty that evening, Joey was leaving her house. Her sister stopped her by the door.

At first, Joey looked angry. Was Bessie going to start a quarrel? But Bessie smiled and held up a lipstick.

"Before you leave, let me put some of this on you," Bessie said. "It's a good red color. You'll look great if you wear this."

Joey was surprised. She never wore makeup. She never thought about it. But Bessie was trying to be nice to her. Joey didn't want to make her sister unhappy.

"OK," she said.

Bessie carefully put some of the red makeup on her sister's lips. Then she gave her the lipstick. "You'll probably need it again later—if someone kisses you!" she said. And they both laughed.

———

A few minutes later, the four friends were walking to the movie theater together. Jen was walking with Dawson. Behind them, Joey was walking with Pacey.

Joey didn't want to be there. Jen was trying to be nice to her, but that made Joey angry. Every time Jen said something nice, Joey said something nasty. Why? Well, she didn't want *Jen* to be nice to her. She wanted *Dawson* to be nice to her. And she didn't want him to be nice to Jen.

"Joey, I like your lipstick," Jen said as they stopped in front of the theater. "It looks wonderful on you. What's the name of the color?"

"I don't know," Joey replied. "What's the name of the

color of your hair. It comes from a bottle—I know that!"

"Joey!" Dawson said angrily. "Stop this!"

"Oh, don't worry about me," Jen said. "Joey wants to be nasty to me. I want to make that very difficult for her."

The four friends bought their tickets for the movie.

"Do you want anything to eat?" Dawson asked Jen.

"Yes, will you get me some popcorn, please?" she replied.

Dawson bought some popcorn for Jen. Then they all went into the theater and sat down. Jen sat down first, then Dawson sat beside her. Joey sat between Dawson and Pacey.

Pacey looked around. After a few seconds, he saw Tamara Jacobs. She was sitting in a seat near the front of the theater. Next to her was an empty seat. She was keeping the seat for him!

Pacey stood up.

"I'll be back soon," he told the others.

At that moment, someone started switching off the lights in the theater. The film was beginning. Joey saw Dawson move his left hand towards Jen's right hand. Soon, his hand was covering her hand.

"Oh, Jen," Joey said. "Are you going to kiss Dawson later? You must be very good at it. You must have kissed hundreds of guys. You had lots of practice kissing boys when you lived in New York!"

Dawson stood up suddenly. He grabbed Joey's arm and held it tightly. He was very angry.

"Come outside for a moment, Joey," he said. "We have to talk about something!"

"Be quiet!" said a man behind them. "We can't hear the movie. Sit down and be quiet!"

Dawson pulled Joey out of the theater.

"What's wrong with you, Joey?" Dawson shouted. The two young people were standing in the street. "You have a problem. What is it?"

"Oh, are you speaking to me now, Dawson?" Joey replied. She was angry too. "You haven't spoken to me this evening. Your new blond friend arrived in this town. Then you stopped speaking to me. *That's* my problem, Dawson. You only think about her and you behave badly to everyone else."

"OK—yes, I talk to Jen," Dawson said. "Is that wrong? I like her. Why aren't you pleased about that? Aren't you my friend any longer? Don't you want me to be happy? Don't you understand me any more?"

"Oh, Dawson," Joey said. Suddenly she felt very tired. "I understand you. I understand you very well. I have always understood you. And now, I'm going to *stop* understanding you. I'm going home!"

Joey turned and walked away.

———

Pacey sat down in the empty seat next to Tamara Jacobs.

"Hi, Tamara," he said.

"Pacey, what are you doing here?" Miss Jacobs asked him. She looked surprised. Then she looked worried.

"I came with some friends," Pacey replied.

"Oh, that's good," Miss Jacobs said. Suddenly she smiled. "It's good to see you. But why aren't you sitting with your friends?"

"Well, I *came* with some friends," Pacey said. "But I don't want to sit with them. I want to sit with you. Why are you surprised? You invited me to come to the movie. It was your idea."

31

"Pacey, you don't understand," Miss Jacobs said. "When we talked earlier, you misunderstood me."

At that moment, a middle-aged man came up to them. He was Ben Gold, the teacher of film class at Capeside High. He was carrying a large box of popcorn. He looked angry.

"Is this kid making trouble, Tamara?" he asked.

"Be quiet!" said a man who was sitting behind them.

"No, Ben," Miss Jacobs said. "He isn't making trouble. He's a boy from one of my classes. He saw me here and he came to say hello."

"Well, you're sitting in my seat, kid," Ben Gold said.

"It's not your seat," Pacey said angrily. "Tamara invited me to come to the movie."

"That isn't true, Ben," Miss Jacobs said. "Pacey didn't understand something that I said. He got the wrong idea."

"Be quiet! Sit down and be *quiet!*" the man behind them said. "I can't hear the movie."

Ben Gold grabbed Pacey's arm and pulled him from the seat.

"You must find another place to sit," he said. "I'll help you. Stand up."

Suddenly, Pacey pulled his arm away from Mr Gold. The teacher fell forward. His popcorn flew out of the box, into the air. Most of the popcorn fell on the angry man who was sitting behind Miss Jacobs.

The angry man stood up. He was very big. He hit Pacey in the face—he hit Pacey very hard.

5

Almost a Kiss

Dawson and Jen were standing near the front door of Jen's house. The two young people had walked home together from the movie theater.

"Jen, I'm sorry about this evening," Dawson said. "It was terrible!"

"Yes, it *was* terrible," Jen replied. "But that wasn't your fault, Dawson. It was *my* fault."

"No, Jen," Dawson said. "I made a date with you. Joey was angry and upset about that. She was jealous and she behaved very badly. That wasn't your fault. Pacey decided to flirt with a woman who was more than twenty years older than him. An angry man in the theater hit Pacey. Was anyone surprised about that? No. And *that* wasn't your fault. *Nothing* was your fault."

Dawson looked at Jen. He wanted to kiss her very much. But he was worried. He did not want her to laugh at him. And he did not want her to be angry with him.

"Everything was *my* fault, not yours," he went on. "I thought, 'Jen won't make a date with me unless Joey and Pacey are with us too.' Joey didn't want to come to the movie this evening. I asked her to come because I wanted to be with you. And I asked her to come because I wanted someone to be with Pacey. Joey came because she wanted to please me. But she was very unhappy—why didn't I guess that? I don't understand people very well. I'm not good at understanding people."

"You're wrong Dawson," Jen said quietly. "You understand people very well. And you understand yourself.

You're kind, and you care about people. You care about other people's feelings. You're handsome but you aren't arrogant. You aren't selfish and pleased with yourself. You're a very loveable person."

Dawson moved closer to Jen. He looked at her soft mouth. He was going to kiss her.

But at that moment, someone switched on a light by the door of Jen's house.

"Is that you, Jen?" a voice called. "You must come in now."

"That's my grandmother. I have to go," Jen said quietly. "Goodnight, Dawson."

———

Pacey was standing on the boardwalk beside the harbor. The moon was very bright. It was shining on the water. The water looked silver in the moonlight.

The harbor was full of boats. A few of them were fishing boats. But most of them were expensive pleasure boats. People spent their vacations on these boats. The boats belonged to the rich tourists who visited Capeside in the summer.

"The people who own boats like these are rich and *happy*," Pacey told himself. "Will *I* ever be happy?"

Pacey didn't feel very happy at that moment. It was late. His face was very painful. And he was angry. He thought about Tamara Jacobs.

"I *didn't* get the wrong idea," he said to himself. "I didn't misunderstand Tamara. I *knew* what she wanted. She told me, '*Summer of '42* is my favorite film.' And she was telling me something else. She *wanted* to meet me at the movie theater. She *was* flirting with me!"

And as Pacey thought about the pretty teacher, he saw her. She was walking along the boardwalk. She was coming towards him. He turned his face away and looked at the harbor again. But she stopped next to him.

"Pacey, I was worried about you," Miss Jacobs said. "I'm sorry about this evening. You got the wrong idea about me. I didn't want that to happen."

"Forget about it," Pacey replied unhappily. He turned and started to walk away. But Miss Jacobs grabbed his arm.

"Please, Pacey," she said. "Don't be angry. Talk to me for a minute."

"What do you want to talk about?" Pacey said. "Do you want to talk about *Summer of '42* or do you want to talk about *The Graduate?*"

"Pacey, you got the wrong idea," Tamara said. "You misunderstood me."

"No, Miss Jacobs," Pacey said angrily. "I got the *right* idea. You wanted me to flirt with you. You're much older than me. You're worried about that. You thought, 'I'll find a stupid, ugly, lonely boy and I'll flirt with him. That will make me feel young. His feelings aren't important. He's only a kid!' That's what you thought."

Suddenly he stopped. Why had he said these terrible things? He was a fool. Now Tamara was never going to speak to him again.

Tamara Jacobs put her hands gently on Pacey's face.

"You're wrong about one thing, Pacey," she said quietly. "You aren't a stupid, ugly boy. You're a very fine young man."

And she kissed his lips. It was a long, soft kiss. Then suddenly, she turned away from him.

"I'm—I'm sorry," she said. "That was wrong—it was

35

very wrong. Please forgive me. And please forget about the kiss. Goodnight, Pacey." She walked away quickly.

"Goodnight—Miss Jacobs!" Pacey shouted. "I'll see you in class."

"Maybe she doesn't understand herself," Pacey thought. "But she enjoyed kissing me—I know that."

———

At school the next day, Dawson was talking to some of the other boys between classes. As they talked, they heard a voice on the school's loudspeakers. It was a girl's voice.

"Don't forget about the dance on Saturday evening," the girl said. "It will be the best day of the school year! The school football team has a very important game on Saturday. We all want them to win. And they *will* win—we're sure of that. So come to the dance on Saturday evening and celebrate their win. Make a date with someone now. Don't forget, everyone. Buy your tickets today!"

"Are you going to the dance?" one of the boys asked Dawson.

"No, I never go to dances," Dawson replied. "I hate dancing. Joey Potter always comes to my house on Saturday evenings. We always watch movies together. And that's what I'll be doing this Saturday. Watching movies by Steven Spielberg is better than dancing!"

———

At lunchtime, Dawson, Joey, Jen, and Pacey sat together.

"We have to work on my film again this weekend," Dawson told the others. "And this time, Joey, you must kiss Pacey. You mustn't say no again."

"Dawson, listen to me," Joey replied. "I've tried to help you with this film. I *always* try to help you. But there's one thing that I will never do. I will *not* kiss Pacey. I'll kiss a snake. I'll kiss a fish. But I won't kiss Pacey. Do you understand?"

Dawson looked at her and he looked at Pacey. Then he looked at Jen.

"OK, I have a new idea," he said to his three friends. "In my story for the movie, you die at the end, Joey. Pacey cuts off your head in the last scene. But now I have a better idea. Now, he kills you in the middle of the film. We'll be able to use the rubber head. After that, your cousin from New York arrives in town. She's very clever and very beautiful. She tries to find the person who killed you. Jen will be the cousin from New York. We'll be able to use nearly all the scenes that we've already filmed."

"On Saturday morning, we'll film the scene where Pacey kills Joey," Dawson went on. "I've finished the rubber head now. It looks great. After that, Joey won't be in any more scenes. When we shoot the rest of the movie, she can help me with the camera and the lights. We can still finish all the filming on Saturday. What do you think about my new idea?"

"OK, I'll act in your film, Dawson," Jen said.

"That's a great idea," Pacey said, smiling. "Now I won't have to kiss Joey. I'll have to kiss Jen." He looked at Jen happily.

But suddenly, Dawson looked unhappy.

"Well, no," he said. "Maybe we won't have any kissing in this new story."

Joey laughed. Now Dawson was jealous too—that was good. And she was going to help her friend with the camera and the lights. She liked the idea. It was better than acting in the movie. And she didn't have to kiss Pacey any more. That was best of all!

After the last class that afternoon, Jen was putting some books into her locker. Suddenly she heard a voice behind her. She turned around and she saw a tall, very handsome boy. He was several years older than she was. He had brown hair and a muscular body.

"Hi," the boy said. "My name is Cliff—Cliff Elliot."

"Hi," Jen replied. "I'm Jen—Jen Lindley."

"Jen, that's a nice name," Cliff said. "Do you like dancing, Jen? Will you come to the dance with me on Saturday? I play for the Capeside High football team. We're going to win our game. So will you help me celebrate our win?"

6

The Kissing Lesson

It was Friday evening. Dawson was in the living room of his house. He was looking at the rubber model of Joey Potter's head. Dawson was very good at making models. The model head looked a lot like Joey's head. He looked carefully at the lips. The rubber lips looked a lot like Joey's lips.

Dawson was looking at Joey's lips but he was thinking about Jen's lips.

"I almost kissed Jen on Monday," he said to himself. "Maybe I *will* kiss her soon. But when I do kiss her, I want it to be a good kiss. I don't know anything about kissing girls. What's the best way to kiss someone—someone who you like very much? I don't know. But I want Jen to remember our first kiss. I want her to remember it forever. So I need some information about kissing. Who can help me with this? Pacey doesn't know anything about kissing girls."

At that moment, Dawson's father came into the room.

"Hi, Son," Mitch Leery said. "That model head is great. Have you almost finished shooting the scenes for your movie? Do you want any help with it?"

"Hi, Dad," Dawson said. "Thanks, but I don't need any help with the movie. We'll finish shooting it on Saturday. But—er—there *is* something that you can help me with. I need some information. I want to know about the best way to kiss a girl. What's the right way to do it? I'm— I'm worried about this."

Mitch smiled and laughed quietly. "When I was fifteen, I worried about kissing too," he said. "But there isn't a right way to kiss a girl, Dawson. You put your lips on her lips. If *she* likes it and *you* like it, then you did it the right way! The only information that I can give you is this. When you kiss someone, you mustn't think about anything else. You must empty your mind.

And the girl must empty her mind too. It will only be really good when you've had some practice. But there are some simple rules. Try kissing the model head, Dawson. I'll tell you if you do something wrong."

Mitch Leery held up the rubber model of Joey Potter's head.

"Rule One—your lips mustn't be dry, Dawson," he said. "Make your lips wet with your tongue."

Dawson moved his tongue over his lips. Then he carefully kissed the model head on the lips.

"That's right," his father told him. "When you've had a little practice, you'll be great! Now try that again."

———

Joey walked quietly into Dawson's house. The front door was open and Joey didn't ring the doorbell. She came to Dawson's house whenever she wanted to come. She had been doing this for many years. She didn't have to ask anyone about it.

Today, she wanted to see her friend very much.

"I was unkind to him on Monday," she said, "I need to talk to him about my feelings."

She moved quietly through the house. Outside the living room, she stopped. The door was open. Dawson and his father were inside the room. They hadn't heard Joey come into the house. Dawson was looking at a rubber model of her own head. Mr Leery was holding the head in front of his son's face.

Suddenly, Dawson started to kiss the model on the lips.

"That's great!" Mr Leery said. "Now do it again, but close your eyes this time. That's Rule Two. Always close your eyes!"

Dawson closed his eyes and he kissed the rubber model

of Joey's head again.

"He's kissing *me*," Joey thought. "Dawson wants to kiss me. He's asking his father about the best way to kiss me!"

For a few seconds, she felt very happy. But then she had another thought.

"No, that's wrong," she told herself. Suddenly she felt very sad. "Dawson doesn't want to kiss me. He wants to kiss Jen Lindley. He's asking his father about the best way to kiss Jen."

Suddenly, Joey no longer wanted to talk to Dawson about her feelings. Very quietly, she turned and walked back to the front door. And very quietly, she left the house.

7

A Change of Plan

On Saturday morning, Dawson, Pacey, Joey, and Jen worked on Dawson's horror movie. They filmed five scenes on a boardwalk by the harbor. The first scene was the one where Pacey cut off Joey's head with a big knife. Dawson filmed Pacey holding the knife above his head. Then Dawson moved closer to his friend and filmed a close-up of the knife. Next he filmed Pacey holding up the rubber model of Joey's head. Dawson had put lots of red paint on the neck of the rubber model. It looked horrible! As he filmed, the paint dripped from the neck and fell onto the boardwalk. The paint looked like blood. Dawson bent his body forward and filmed a close-up of the pool of blood on the boardwalk.

The other four scenes were the last scenes of the movie. Jen acted in all of them and Joey helped Dawson with the lights.

By lunchtime, they had finished all the filming. Now Dawson had to put all the scenes together—he had to edit the final video tape. He was going to do that during the next two weeks. When he'd edited the film, he was going to send it to Boston.

"Thank you, everybody," Dawson said. "This movie is going to be great!"

Dawson put his camera in its case.

"I'll walk home with you, Jen," he said.

Jen and Dawson walked away together. Pacey and Joey watched them go.

"Are you going to the school dance this evening, Pacey?" Joey asked. "Which teachers will be there? Do you know?"

"Well, yes, Miss Jacobs will be there—I know that," Pacey replied. "And I'm going. The woman that I dream about will be there. Are you going to the dance, Joey?"

"No," Joey said. "I'm going to watch videos of Dawson's favorite movies at Dawson's house. It will be like every other Saturday evening!"

She didn't ask Pacey about the woman of his dreams. She didn't want to know who it was. "It isn't me, so that's OK!" she thought.

She walked towards her little rowboat. "I'll see you on Monday," she called to Pacey.

———

Jen and Dawson stopped near the front door of Jen's house. They looked at each other. They were both thinking about the evening when they almost kissed. And as they thought about the kiss that didn't happen, they both smiled.

"What are you going to do this evening?" Dawson asked. "Joey is coming to my house. We're going to watch some movies. Can you come too?"

"Oh, I'm sorry, Dawson," Jen replied. "Joey doesn't want to spend time with me. And I can't come to your house this evening. I'm going to the school dance."

Dawson's smile disappeared. Suddenly, he felt very sad.

"Who's going to take you to the dance?" he asked quietly.

"Oh, someone who I met last week," Jen replied. "He plays for the Capeside football team. His name is Cliff Elliot."

Cliff Elliot—the brown-haired guy with muscles who attended the film class! The boy who Mr Gold was helping with his stupid film about football!

Jen looked at Dawson's face.

"Don't be sad," she said. "I didn't know about your plan. And I do want to meet more people from school. I didn't really make a date with Cliff. He asked me to go to the dance with him and I said OK."

"That's called making a date," Dawson said.

Jen thought for a moment.

"Yes, you're right," she said. "I'm sorry, Dawson. I wanted to have some fun this weekend."

Then she thought again.

"I have an idea," she said. "You could come to the dance too. We could dance together a few times. I don't have to stay with Cliff all evening."

"No, I won't do that," Dawson replied. "I'll stay at home and watch movies."

And as he walked to his own door, he was thinking about all the things that had happened that week.

"What happened to the kiss that we almost had?" he asked himself.

———

It was Saturday evening. Joey and Dawson were sitting on the bed in Dawson's room. But they weren't watching a movie. Dawson was talking and Joey was listening. Dawson was talking about Cliff Elliot.

"His football film is so stupid!" he said. "Why is Mr Gold helping him? There are hundreds of movies about football. They all have the same story. They're all about a player who gets injured in a game. The injured player always continues to play in the game. He always scores the final points in the game. The world does *not* need another movie about that stupid story!"

He stopped speaking for a moment.

"Why does Jen want to go to the dance with Cliff Elliot?" he asked, more quietly. "What reasons does she have?"

Joey laughed and looked at her friend.

"Well, Cliff is handsome," she replied. "And he's tall and strong. He has a nice body. And he's two years older than us. And he drives a car. Are those enough reasons? I'll think of some others—"

Joey was angry. She was trying to make Dawson angry too. But then, she couldn't say anything more. Suddenly, he looked so unhappy.

Dawson was unhappy because he was jealous. Joey knew about jealousy. She had been feeling jealous all that week. She had started feeling jealous when Dawson saw Jen getting out of the taxi. Now everything in Joey's life was horrible! She loved Dawson, but he didn't love her. And now Dawson loved Jen, but Jen had made a date with

"Well, Cliff is handsome," she replied. "And he's tall and strong—"

Cliff. Dawson was unhappy about that. Joey was sad because Dawson was sad. It was like a bad movie!

"What did Cliff Elliot do?" Dawson asked her. "He's with Jen this evening. Why? He did something that I *didn't* do. What was it?"

"He asked Jen to go to the dance with him, Dawson," Joey replied. "You *didn't* ask her. It's not difficult to understand—it's very simple."

Suddenly Dawson stood up. "I'm going to the dance," he said. "Will you come with me?"

"You want to watch Jen dancing with another guy?" she said. "Are you crazy, Dawson?"

"What else can I do?" he asked. "Maybe when she sees me—" he stopped.

Joey looked at him. She hated seeing him like this.

"OK, Dawson," she said quietly. "I'll come. But it won't be fun."

8

At The Dance

The Capeside High football team had won their game. Everyone at the dance was celebrating—everyone except Pacey. He was standing by a wall in the school gymnasium. He wasn't watching the hundreds of happy teenagers who were dancing. He was watching the woman of his dreams. Tamara Jacobs was talking to Ben Gold. She was wearing a dark blue dress. She looked wonderful. And she looked happy.

A few seconds later, Mr Gold walked away. He went to

talk to someone else.

"Will Tamara be happy to see me?" Pacey asked himself. "Maybe she *will* be happy. Maybe this will be the best night of my life. Well, I'll soon know about that."

Quickly, he walked up to the beautiful English teacher.

"Hello, Miss Jacobs," he said. "How are you?"

"Oh, Pacey—hello," Miss Jacobs said. She didn't look happy now. "I'm fine. How are *you* this evening?"

"I want to talk to you," Pacey said. "I want to talk about our relationship. Will you dance with me?"

"No, Pacey, that's not a good idea," Miss Jacobs said. "And we don't *have* a relationship!" She was worried—Pacey could see that.

"I'm a teacher here," she continued. "Please remember that."

"Did *you* remember that when you kissed me?" Pacey asked.

"I have to talk to someone now, Pacey," Miss Jacobs said. "I'm sorry. Goodbye."

And she walked quickly away.

———

Dawson and Joey stood by the doorway of the gymnasium. Large pieces of brightly colored cloth were hanging from the ceiling. Someone had painted pictures of huge fish on the pieces of cloth. Brightly colored lights shone around the walls. Dawson and Joey were watching the happy young people who were dancing. Joey smiled when she heard the music. Old songs by the Beach Boys were still popular in Capeside!

Soon Joey and Dawson saw Jen. She was dancing with Cliff Elliot. They danced very well together. They were smiling at each other.

"We have to do something quickly," Dawson said.

"Dawson, here is a correction," Joey replied. "*You* have to do something quickly. This isn't my problem."

"You *have* to help me," Dawson said. "Do you dance, Joey?"

"No, Dawson," said Joey. "I don't dance—you know that. I *never* dance!"

"Well, this is the first night of the rest of your life," said Dawson. "Tonight, you must dance."

He grabbed Joey's arm and he pulled her into the middle of the room.

"Dawson, you *are* crazy," Joey said quietly. She was not happy. But she tried to dance with him. And she tried to smile.

After a few minutes, Dawson whispered in her ear.

"Joey, you're good at this," he said softly.

Then suddenly, Jen and Cliff were dancing beside them.

"Hi," Jen said to Dawson. "You came to the dance. I'm pleased."

Dawson wanted to speak. But he couldn't think of any words.

Jen smiled at him. "This is Cliff!" she said. "Cliff, these are my friends, Joey and Dawson."

And a few seconds later, Cliff and Jen were dancing on the other side of the room.

_____

Half an hour later, Dawson met Jen outside the gymnasium. She was alone. Joey was talking to some friends and Dawson had wanted to get away from the noise of the music for a few minutes.

"Hi, Dawson," Jen said. "Can we dance together now?"

"Where's Cliff?" Dawson asked.

"Oh, do you want to dance with Cliff?" Jen asked. "Don't you want to dance with me?" She laughed.

But Dawson didn't laugh. He wasn't happy.

"Well, you made a date with Cliff," he said angrily. "I don't understand your reasons. But he's the boy that you really like. He has muscles and money but he isn't intelligent. Maybe he doesn't want you to dance with me."

"OK, Dawson," Jen replied. Now she was angry too. "If you don't want to dance with me, that's great! Goodbye."

She walked quickly away.

Dawson watched her go.

"I'm a fool," he told himself. "Jen asked me to dance with her. Did I say yes? No, I didn't. I said some angry jealous words about Cliff instead."

He walked towards the gymnasium.

———

Joey was looking for Dawson. She couldn't see him anywhere. But she saw Pacey coming towards her. He was looking for someone too.

Pacey came up to Joey and grabbed her arm. Then he whispered in her ear.

"Joey, you have to dance with me," he said quickly. Suddenly, Joey's body felt cold. She remembered the day when Pacey had tried to kiss her. She didn't want to dance with him now. She didn't want Pacey to hold her in his arms. But he had been her friend for a long time. She tried to be nice to him.

"Pacey, you're very kind," she said. "But I don't dance. And please don't hurt my arm."

Pacey pulled her to the center of the room. Couples were dancing slowly to a sad song.

"You *have* to dance with me!" he told her. "I want to make Tamara jealous. She won't dance with me. But if she sees me dancing with you, she'll be jealous. Then she'll be nice to me."

"No, Pacey," Joey said. "Leave me alone."

But Pacey started to dance. And he held Joey very tightly in his arms. She had to dance with him.

"I hate you," she told him.

"Please, Joey," Pacey said. "This is important to me. I'll give you some money if you'll dance with me. Maybe you'll hate me for the rest of your life. But please dance with me now."

At that moment, they danced past Miss Jacobs. Suddenly, Pacey pulled Joey closer to him. And he kissed her on the lips.

Joey stopped moving. Her face became red. Her skin became hot. She was very, very angry. She hit Pacey on one side of his face. Then she hit him on the other side. She hit him very hard. After that, she turned and ran out of the room.

Pacey looked around the room. Everybody was looking at him. And Miss Jacobs had seen everything that had happened!

——————

Dawson was standing by the wall of the gymnasium. He was watching the dancers. Where was Joey? He didn't know. He hadn't seen her for some time. But Jen was danc-ing with Cliff again.

"If I don't do something soon, I'm going to lose Jen," he thought. "She'll be Cliff's girlfriend. She won't make any more dates with me. She'll make dates with Cliff and she'll tell me about them every day. I'll be Jen's friend—the one who she tells about her boyfriends. But I won't be *her* boyfriend. If my life is a movie, this is a very bad movie. I'm going to write some new scenes!"

The music stopped for a few moments, and people stopped dancing. Before the music started again, Dawson moved quickly. Suddenly, he was standing next to Jen and Cliff. He grabbed Cliff's arm and pulled him away from Jen.

"Goodbye, Cliff," he said. "It's time to say goodnight. Thanks for bringing Jen to the dance. But I'm going to dance with her now. And I'm going to dance with her for the rest of the evening."

Cliff was very surprised. Jen was surprised too.

"Dawson, what are you doing?" she asked him.

"That's a good question," Cliff said. "What *are* you doing?"

"I'm going to dance with Jen," Dawson said.

Cliff looked at Jen.

"Do you *want* to be with this—person?"

She didn't answer. She looked at Cliff. Then she looked at Dawson. But she didn't speak. She didn't have anything to say.

"She doesn't want to dance with you, Leery," Cliff said. "She's *my* girlfriend." He was very angry. "You have to leave now. If you don't, I'll—"

"No, she's *my* girlfriend." Dawson said. "And *you* have to leave!" He was angry too.

But Jen was angrier than both of them.

"This is so stupid!" she shouted. "You're both behaving like little kids. I'll leave. Then you won't have a problem!"

Then she turned and left the room.

9

The Beginning of Everything Else

Joey, Dawson, and Pacey were walking together along the street. Dawson was in the middle. Joey didn't want to be near Pacey.

The evening had been terrible. It had been like a terrible movie. But Dawson hadn't watched the scene between Pacey and Joey. He didn't understand why they weren't talking to each other. He was thinking about his own problems.

Soon, Pacey turned off the street. He was going towards the harbor.

"Goodnight," he said quietly.

"Goodnight," Dawson answered. Joey didn't speak. The two friends walked on in silence.

After a minute, Dawson had to say something.

"Joey, why did you leave me alone at the dance?" he asked. "I was so stupid. I behaved so badly."

"It wasn't *my* fault, Dawson," Joey replied. "Growing up brings problems for all of us. We're all learning about life. You know that."

"Well, what have we learned from this evening?" Dawson asked.

"In the future, we must stay at home on Saturday evenings and watch movies. That's what we've learned!" Joey replied.

"That won't be difficult," Dawson said. "My relationship with Jen is finished."

"Dawson, you never started a real relationship with her," Joey said.

"You're right," Dawson replied sadly.

But at that moment, they both saw Jen. She was sitting near the edge of the creek. She was looking down at the water.

Dawson looked at Joey. She looked at him. She had never felt so sad in all her life.

"It's OK, Dawson," she said. "Go to her, if you want to. Maybe your movie will have a happy ending."

———

Pacey was by the harbor. He was sitting in a rowboat. He was looking at the water and the lights on the pleasure boats.

He was feeling very sad. Everything had gone wrong. Pacey wasn't lucky in his relationships with girls—he knew that. He always said the wrong things to them.

But tonight he had been very stupid.

He thought about Joey. She had been his friend for many years. But she had hated him when he had kissed her. No, he wasn't lucky with girls. And now there was someone who he really liked. Someone who had kissed him. Someone who had *liked* kissing him—he was sure of that. But she wasn't a girl. She was a woman and she was his English teacher. Could anything be worse than this?

And as he was thinking about Miss Jacobs, he heard her voice behind him.

"Pacey? Are you OK?"

"No, Miss Jacobs," Pacey replied. "I'm not OK. I'm very unhappy. Everything in my life is wrong. You know that. Why are you here?"

"Pacey," Miss Jacobs said gently. "I came here to look for you. I've made you unhappy and I'm sorry. I wanted to tell you that. You're unhappy and that's *my* fault. I kissed you and I flirted with you. That was wrong. I've had a lot of problems in my life. And now I've done something very stupid and I've made you unhappy. I feel terrible about that. But your life will change, Pacey. It will get better. Being fifteen is very difficult. But life *will* get better. Please believe me."

"Don't be sorry about kissing me, Tamara," Pacey said. "It wasn't all your fault. It was my fault too. You kissed me, but I kissed you. Don't be sorry about it."

Miss Jacobs looked into his eyes and she smiled at him.

"OK, but it can't happen again, Pacey," she said. "You have to understand that. Goodnight. Try to be happy."

And then she turned and walked away.

———

Dawson stood next to Jen. For a few minutes, they looked out over the water without speaking. The only sound in the night was some quiet music. It was coming from one of the boats in the creek.

At last Dawson spoke.

"Jen, I'm sorry," he said. "I'm very, very sorry."

"You made me angry tonight," Jen replied.

"I know that," Dawson said. "I was afraid, Jen. I thought, 'I'm going to lose Jen. Cliff will be her boyfriend. She wants me to be her special friend and not her boyfriend. Joey is my special friend, and now I'm going to be Jen's special friend. Jen will tell me about her feelings for other boys. She'll tell me about her boyfriends, but I'll never be one of them.' That's what I thought. That's why I was afraid."

Jen stood up and looked into Dawson's eyes.

"Do you *want* to be my boyfriend, Dawson?" Jen asked quietly.

"Yes," he replied. "Do you want me to be your boyfriend?"

"Let's try it," Jen said. "Maybe it's a good idea."

Dawson smiled. And he gently kissed Jen's lips.

"We spent the evening at the school dance," he said. "But we never danced together. Shall we dance together now? We have music from the boat."

And a moment later, the two young people were dancing beside the creek in the bright moonlight.

Points for Understanding

1

1 Dawson is going to make a model head from rubber. Why?
2 "Nothing *has* to change," Dawson says. He is sad. Why is he sad?

2

Pacey says, "Tamara wants me! She was flirting with me." Why does he think this?

3

1 When Dawson hears about Cliff Elliot's movie, he is angry. Why?
2 Who is Grams?

4

"You misunderstood me," Miss Jacobs tells Pacey. Why does she think this?

5

1 "Joey didn't want to come to the movie this evening," Dawson tells Jen. Is he right? Why *has* Joey come with them?
2 "You wanted to feel young again," Pacey tells Miss Jacobs. Why does he believe this?

6

What are Mitch Leery's two rules for kissing?

7

1 Dawson films a close-up of a pool of red paint. Why does he do this?
2 In the evening, Joey tries to make Dawson angry. Why?

8

1 Why does Dawson want Joey to dance with him?
2 "Oh, do you want to dance with Cliff?" Jen asks Dawson. Why does she say this?
3 Why does Pacey kiss Joey?

9

"Maybe your movie will have a happy ending," Joey tells Dawson. Why does she say this?

There are other

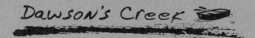

stories in the Macmillan Guided Readers Series
at Elementary Level:

Dawson's Creek: Long Hot Summer
K. S. Rodriguez
Retold by F. H. Cornish

A specially adapted version for Macmillan Guided Readers of the second story—based on the TV show "Dawson's Creek™" created by Kevin Williamson—that follows the lives and loves of a group of teenage friends growing up in a small New England coastal town.

Summer vacation. Dawson pursues his amateur film career with the reluctant help of Joey and Pacey.
Jen enrols in lifeguarding classes and Pacey joins her, thinking that this will be an excellent way to meet girls.
Believing Dawson is now Jen's boyfriend, Joey makes him jealous by meeting other boys. Who will Dawson choose?

64pp

 0 333 97317 8

 0 333 97318 6

 0 333 97319 4

Availability: World, ex. US, its territories and dependencies, Canada & Australia
™ and © 2002 Columbia TriStar Television, Inc. All Rights Reserved

Dawson's Creek: Shifting Into Overdrive
C. J. Anders
Retold by F. H. Cornish

A specially adapted version for Macmillan Guided Readers of the third story—based on the TV show "Dawson's Creek™", created by Kevin Williamson—that follows the lives and loves of a group of teenage friends growing up in a small New England coastal town.

Angered by Dawson's indecision, Joey and Jen form a reluctant alliance and plan a weekend together in New York to attend the sixteenth birthday party of Jen's cousin.

Joey is amazed on her first visit to the Big Apple. And Jen shows her the lifestyle that she left behind when her absentee parents sent her to live in Capeside with her strict grandmother.

Dawson and Pacey have their own plans and after "borrowing" his father's truck, Pacey offers to drive the two of them to New York to surprise the girls. When they gatecrash the lavish birthday party, things get wild.

64pp

 0 333 97320 8

 0 333 97321 6

 0 333 97322 4

Availability: World, ex. US, its territories and dependencies, Canada & Australia

Dawson's Creek:
Major Meltdown
K. S. Rodriguez
Retold by F. H. Cornish

A specially adapted version for Macmillan Guided Readers
of the fourth story—based on the TV show "Dawson's
Creek™", created by Kevin Williamson—that follows the
lives and loves of a group of teenage friends growing up in
a small New England coastal town.

Jen invites her friends to stay the weekend in her parents'
ski cabin in the mountains.

Joey persuades her sister to give her time off from helping
in the family restaurant.

Pacey and Dawson get the weekend free from working in
the local video store, and eagerly anticipate meeting girls
on the slopes.

But Dawson is thrown into turmoil. He realizes the depth
of his feelings for Joey, but cannot resist Jen.

Pacey is literally bowled over by a local girl, and to his
friends' amazement starts to talk of leaving his home and
school in Capeside.

64pp

  0 333 97323 2

  0 333 97324 0

  0 333 97325 9

Availability: World, ex. US, its territories and dependencies, Canada & Australia

Published by Macmillan Heinemann ELT
Between Towns Road, Oxford OX4 3PP
Macmillan Heinemann ELT is an imprint of
Macmillan Publishers Limited
Companies and representatives throughout the world
Heinemann is a registered trademark of Harcourt Education, used under licence.

ISBN 1–405072–60–1
EAN 978–1–405072–60–1

First published 1998 by Pocket Books, a division of Simon and Schuster
Inc., New York
First published in Great Britain by Channel 4 Books, an imprint of
Macmillan Publishers Ltd, 1999

This specially adapted and retold version by F. H. Cornish
for Macmillan Readers
First published 2002

This edition first published 2005

Illustrations on pages 8 and 9 by Maureen Gray
Original cover template design by Jackie Hill
Cover design by Herringbone Design

Printed in Thailand

2009 2008 2007 2006
10 9 8 7 6 5 4 3